The Paperback Psychic Predictions:

2021 and Beyond

By Tanya Psi

The Paperback Psychic Predictions: 2021 and Beyond

December 2019

All rights reserved.

Copyright © 2019 by Tanya Psi

Published in Toronto, Ontario.

"We are all one under the sun."
--- Tanya Psi

TABLE OF CONTENTS

Introduction — 5

Technology Predictions — 6

Health Predictions — 10

Entertainment Predictions — 11

World Predictions — 12

Final Words — 23

INTRODUCTION

My goal for this book is to let you know about potential future outcomes in the world. Whether you take it as truth is your own choice.

I am a fourth generation psychic. For fear of being outed for practicing obeah or plain ass being crazy, I am using a pen name to publish my predictions.

Not everyone believes that some can see the future, but since you are reading this, you must be a believer. That or a skeptic. Or maybe the "Simpson's" predictions phenomenon has you curious about what is fluid or set in stone in the future. Either way, you're in for a while ride in this first edition of my never before published predictions.

TECHNOLOGY PREDICTIONS

As of this writing it is November 2019. Actually there are only a few days left until December 2019. The point is, three years from now, there will be a new form of internet. It is being prepped right now as we speak so don't think you can go out and try to make a buck off of this idea...

The new internet is taking away with it Google. Yup, no more google searches. Google has single-handedly ruined the internet... but this book isn't about my issue with the current state of the internet. It's about predictions, and because the internet in its current form as we know it is dying, this book is available in all forms, including paperback.

There will be new ways of searching. There will be sections as I may call them for simplicity. One section is People, Places and Things. There's also a section where all searches will be factual, fact-checked, educational resources and content. There's also another section for entertainment (i.e. shows, music, films). And of course the old internet will be around as it actually cannot be deleted. What a history book!

So back to Google as a company and service. This means all things connected to Google will go way of the dodo bird. No more YouTube, no more Gmail, Google Ads, Google Analytics, Fitbit, you get the drift...

And three to seven years from this writing, Facebook and all of its other companies will be no more. Zuckerberg will end up going to jail. Who knew FB would outlast Google?

And what is the other big tech giant today? Apple of course. Oh Apple Mac what will happen to you?

As a conglomerate, Apple will be sticking around for a few more years as of this writing, as their business model is not as sustainable as people are seeing right now. iPhones will stop being mass produced for one and they will get out of the hardware game, focus on software and entertainment, but then will need to pivot to stay afloat. They will need to pick up a whole new industry to survive. It's a new ballgame out there and it's not a pretty one. With that said, Apple will not be able to pivot and will eventually go the way of the dodo bird. Why? Aint nobody alive with enough money to buy out Apple.

What will our cell phones look like then? If there are no iPhones? By the time iPhone production ceases, technology will be further along and new and improved ways to talk to people will be available to us. You think payphones look archaic? Flip phones? Motorola razers? iPhones will look like that too compared to the holographic phone lines we'll be hooked up to.

And TV? Oh boy, don't get me started on TV! Movie theatres! Computer screens! How will we digest media in the future? The medium is the future. There will be one medium for all entertainment purposes to cut down on waste. Electronic waste. Talk about Big Brother screens in public being watched. Dundas Square... Times Square anyone?

Does this mean we will consume all our media in public? No. There are personal devices that will connect to Big Brother screens around the world. Dubai to Dublin.

Will things be able to be downloaded to our brains? Of course. Think of it as your own personal device. It can and will get a virus though if you aren't careful.

Fear not though, the brain will not be injected with anything to function as a medium conductor.

HEALTH PREDICTIONS

There will be many health breakthroughs in the not so distant future. Namely, cancer cures. But what else?

Blindness will be cured eventually, 10 to 15 years from the writing of this book.

Will mental illness be cured? In our lifetime, only one will have a 50% cure rate: schizophrenia. It will have a highly controversial treatment but the success margins aren't dismal within a 15 year period.

AIDS will not be cured but HIV will be cured in 20 years time.

Type 1 Diabetes will have a cure faster than Type 2 Diabetes.

ENTERTAINMENT PREDICTIONS

Now it's time for my favourite type of predictions. Entertainment. Not just for entertainment purposes either.

Let me start out by saying there's no more Hollywood in the coming future, say 10 - 15 years. Tinseltown is dead. The limelight has gone sour. People just could care less about modern celebrities at the time when Hollywood ceases to exist. The masses are fed up of having them shove things in their faces. They want to go back to a time where things were simpler - Vaudeville if you will - where performers had **TALENT**. Yup, you heard that right Kardashian and Paris Hilton lovers. Being famous for being famous is on its way out. Child stars and child of stars will have the same meaning eventually too. Psst, I have a whole book dedicated to celebrities FYI.

WORLD PREDICTIONS

World predictions... I was reading the news the other day and some guy complained that the world economy isn't running fairly enough. And he couldn't be more right.

In the future, billionaires (minus Kylie Jenner as she will lose her billions just as fast as she made them) will pool their money together becoming richer than before. Because, who understands a billionaire better than a billionaire?

The distance therefore between rich and poor will will reach an all time high before everything comes crashing down. Basically the world market will need to crash in order to build itself back up into a fairer more convenient market **FOR THE PEOPLE**. People will be taken care of from the cradle to the grave. Everyone will be able to afford the necessities. Remember we aren't all trying to get new iPhones by this point. So if you need a house, yes you will get to live in a house. Spacing permitted. Want clothing? Why yes you will have clothing! And food? Well food is at a standstill shortage at this point and lots of people are going back to growing their own food. Guess those 'preppers' were onto something.

Speaking of food, there will be more animal borne diseases that will deplete the supply of things like bacon, pork, beef, fish, basically any and all animal products and byproducts. I guess the vegans and vegetarians were onto something too!

Veganism in the sense of more processed fake foods will take off... again... but this time it is more refined and the strides they have taken in technology help. Yes some people will get sick from veganism so they will need to rely on expensive lab produced meat products. A happy medium in the coming years will be vegetarianism, but there are still issues like salmonella plaguing vegetables and lettuce. The safest bet is veganism if you can stomach it. It will be the more affordable option as there will be ways you can make things at home.

This brings me to transportation. Ok, I didn't have a segue into that, forgive me.

Transportation will be a thing of the past in some areas. No more commuting. No more long line ups. Teleporting is near. Teleporting will be here in 15 years time, and will be perfected up to 40 years from the time of this writing.

In 2025, planes will finally be automated and unmanned. Overtime, the planes' structure gets better but crashes aren't 100 percent eliminated.

What about travel to other countries? Well unfortunately, the world will get more dangerous before it can get better. People will kill tourists for no reason, giving a bad name to the tourist countries. Countries will be on lock down and travel bans will be in place, stranding some people for good, like retirees or people that live in other countries part of the year.

And 25 years from this writing, we will need to wear gas masks outdoors as the environment will be worse for wear, regarding all the pollution surrounding us. Raw sewage will end up in our bodies of water and there will be no way to clean it up. Polar bears will go extinct and the polar ice caps will melt leading to more floods around the world. There will also be more forest fires. Weather-wise there will be more scorching and longer summers, longer and harsher winters in some areas while some places will have no winter at all where they did before. Places that never had snow will have snow as well. It's as if the earth turned on its axis. Which is exactly what is happening. There is no more below the equator and above the equator, in a traditional sense. It too has changed. This does not mean hotter climates will get snow, it just means everything has gotten to be more intense. Think of it as having two equators, one at the North Pole and one in the middle (there's also a dormant third equator that will activate during the end of times when humans have become extinct) and the first equator lost its footing and has moved downwards because the earth's axis shifted. The equator we know has also moved down and is acting as the dormant third in this case. We will be experiencing end of time scorching heat in areas below the equator. People will die due to the extreme heat.

The earth is dying and humans will only be around for the next 100 years (as of this writing).

Speaking of people, there will also be a change to the ways the current governments are set up. There will be a one world government. This does not mean the UN will be in charge. Far from it. The UN is corrupt and will be disbanded. But with this one world government, travel will be much easier than in today's world.

And the way we even buy things will change. Everything will be bought on the internet and there will be no more retail stores due to danger. Things will be fulfilled from warehouses around the world and shipped to people only. So if you work as a retail sales rep, you will be out of a job in the not so distant future.

Jobs as we know them (modern jobs) will cease to exist. New jobs will emerge based upon world needs and we will go back to tried and true manual labour jobs too. FYI keep an eye out for my professions book for a detailed look at current professions and where they will stand in the future.

I know what you're thinking... will self-employment rise? Yes and no. Yes to the extent that you will work for yourself, no in the form of the bureaucracy and red tape.

Will artists be able to survive? Yes and no. I don't think we've really scratched the surface on letting artists make a livable wage from their works and that will not change in the future. With that said, there are more avenues for artists to sell their works or wares. Whether people value it enough to buy them is another issue. So some artists will be successful, while others will not. Just like today. Even with all the opportunities open. People just need to change their mindset but it will not happen in our lifetime.

And another question you're wondering is will we be able to continue to make a living from the internet? No not in its current state. No not in its future state. The internet was meant to be an open source for learning not a monopoly. Yes money can be made, and there will be new forms of monetization BUT and a big but, it will not be enough to make a living off of. People will need to have multiple sources of income. Not just one source anymore. Welcome to the world of an artist!

What about health care? Universal healthcare

will cease to exist. Remember we will be under a one world government in the future. Healthcare will still be around and will be made affordable thanks to Europe. There will be different types of healthcare based on the life stage you are in. For example, eldercare for seniors, childcare for children and so on. Will people in the states and Canada have this affordable new healthcare? Yes, after the fall of their governments. It will be too late for some people though who succumb to their health issues.

Now for beauty. Beauty products will now banned in the coming future if they do not contain organic ingredients as we will have lots of proof toxic beauty ingredients are no good for our bodies.

Clothing... clothing (mass produced, fast fashion), will be a thing of the past. People will learn how to make their own and if they can't or refuse to, they can buy it at cost off of others, like neighbours or friends and family members.

Will there be a WWIII? No. Will there be more wars? Yes. Small wars will exist within countries and places historically at war with each other. That will not change.

Designer babies will be banned. The technology exists but laws ruling not to play god will come about, plus the fact that designer babies increasingly develop more mutations and health issues will put an end to it. Almost like cloning. Will we be able to successfully clone people? No. There's enough people on the planet for one, and there are laws around cloning that will stay intact.

Hair loss will be a thing of the past. No we won't have hair transplants but hair molecules will be able to be grown from the scalp at the cellular level. Think of it as planting a seed and watching the plant grow. This will eliminate baldness.

Will books be a thing of the past? No. Books will continue to stick around in new and old formats until the end of time. Will newspapers cease to exist in the future? Yes.

Deforestation... deforestation will become a predicament. No amount of planting new trees will help. We will need to find a paper alternative in the coming future. Paper as we know it will cease to exist in the next five to 10 years. Recycled paper will still be around but they usually mix it with used and new paper.

What will the new paper alternative be? Unfortunately it will be a plastic source made from microplastics. There will need to be a system in place to keep this new invention out of the landfills but plastic is plastic and will end up in the oceans again anyways. Will there be a better paper alternative that isn't plastic? Yes but that will take 20 - 50 years to come about. The damage is already done. If we could produce something that didn't create waste of any sort, we'd be on our way to a better world. But waste is a byproduct of production in all forms. Will this change? Maybe but it will be too late.

There will be more trade wars before we can agree on free trade between countries.

Supermarkets will cease to exist and prompt a rise in DIY everything.

People will spend more time indoors than ever before in the future. Crime, warfare and pollution are all culprits.

Schools will be a thing of the past in its current form due to the same factors. Children will still be taught, but from home, whether by parents, friends or teachers via the new internet model.

Where does that leave higher education? Distance learning will take off. The world's state will make it impossible for people to study physically at universities and colleges. Not to mention the cost. But just like there is free healthcare with the new government reform, there will be free education.

FINAL WORDS

The future is said to be sometimes fluid and sometimes set in stone. What you have read here can be said to be the same. Some are fluid, as is changeable and some will happen no doubt about it.

I would post a website or an email address but the internet will be changing in a short three years. If you're reading this book in 2023 or after, you most likely wouldn't be able to have much use for them.

So stay tuned to the newer editions I will be releasing in the coming future.

CPSIA information can be obtained
at www.ICGtesting.com
Printed in the USA
LVHW090755310820
664598LV00001B/231